LOST - TRYING TO FIND ANEW

Collected Poems 2023-2024

by David A. Folds

WingSpan Press

Published in the United States and the United Kingdom
by WingSpan Press, Livermore, CA

The WingSpan name, logo and colophon are
the trademarks of WingSpan Publishing.

ISBN 978-1-63683-073-5 (pbk.)
ISBN 978-1-63683-939-4 (ebk.)

First edition 2025

Printed in the United States of America

www.wingspanpress.com

Library of Congress Control Number 2025934849

LOST - TRYING TO FIND ANEW

THIS BOOK IS DEDICATED
TO THE MEMORY OF MY BELOVED WIFE,
VICTORIA (VICKIE) ASTORGA FOLDS, 9/29/46 - 4/2/24.
IT IS ALSO DEDICATED
TO MY BROTHER, CHARLES (CHUCK) FOLDS,
AND HIS WIFE, JANE DEVINE FOLDS,
BOTH HAVING PASSED IN 2024.

New Openings

Lotus in my mind,   petals

-- upper, reaching up for life

-- lower, leaning on the water,

half in, half out

from a placental pool

from life-giving dank

to heat-giving bright.

From the dull, the common

repeated memory of all life,

blossoms appear

that are particular,

that gleam a new shade

declaring another -- the same

-- but another different

creation from me

9/21/1997 - NYC

David A. Folds

Vickie

there is a direct line

from 1979

at the UN Badminton Club

to our lives

together today

one summer evening

I saw her for

the first time

she was on court

and wore

a t-shirt that said

It's Me

somehow then

I knew that it was

this small very pretty

        Philippine lady

who was just being ---

        not full of herself

I got to know

        gradually

when she knew

        I worked in a

            photographic lab

she asked for

        some help

she had a new Nikon

        she could reasonably

          reach forward

she was a little shy

        certainly not aggressive

David A. Folds

after play I would see her

to her uptown bus

days later I asked

for a date

by then her feet were covered

bunion operations on both

we walked eight blocks to

a beautiful Italian movie

"The Tree of Wooden Clogs"

the first steps were taken

towards a lifelong path

we were in it

for the long haul

in it for all tomorrows

8/13/2020 Jersey City, NJ, USA
Reprinted from "Afloat in the Continuum"

Journey

if

a wind flows a breeze

lifts me   transports

me   away

it's as if I

had never

stirred your hand

near mine

still that way

1964 - NYC
Reprinted from "Emotions, Images and Spirit"

David A. Folds

Past the Prime

after a while

    the paint starts to peel

the wood begins

    to warp and chip

cement cracks and buckles

    reshaping itself

and permanent proves

    to be impossible

our skin constantly

    flakes and peels

calcium bones

    having reached their peak

        decline and weaken

and inner organs

    repeat constant work

open to aging

    inconsistencies

with the threat of

    possibilities of failure

will we or have we already

    used our timetable of strength

to advantage

    to reap the bounty

        open before us

while our being can grasp

    the precious moments

that will fly away

    with the wind of time

if we do not embrace

    and cultivate them

3/19/2023 Jersey City, NJ, USA

David A. Folds

Boxes and Pathways

we do live in boxes

little boxes

boxes on top of boxes

cement and steel

wallboard and plaster

inlaid plumbing

and wall hidden wires

pieces put together

our modern prototype

of constructed caves

we travel the routes

connecting one town

to another

with twists and turns

watch other roads

      to the left and right

running parallel

      or veering away at an angle

then we circle

      on to an approach

to a redirecting lane

      to a linking path

leading into our destination

      with a new set of boxes

waiting to open and close

      embracing us without emotion

nature recreated

      by the aggression

      of human nature

4/20/2023 Jersey City, NJ, USA

David A. Folds

A Hope for Healing

off the lonely elevator

in the pristine

sterile hospital

with neutral

non aggressive colors

the passageway

with stories

in each room

that you don't

want to hear

form batteries

of sadness

hoping for renewal

walk in search

of the number

near the open door

entering the room

    feels like some violation

        of protocol or safety

patients in beds

    in a cocoon

        half encased

instruments measuring

    intravenous dosage

others monitoring

    life necessities

everything announcing

    that normal existence

    is in hiatus

David A. Folds

all we can do is

donate our caring

express our love

hoping that progress

will be coming

and regression

will be halted

hoping is all

that is

within our grasp

4/26/2023   Jersey City, NJ, USA

Awake

morning brings to me

    the shock of new oldness

repetition continues

    day after day

but dawn delivers

    coffee fresh sameness

to try to discover

    surprises that stimulate

that try to discover

    a life within focus

afloat

    in a river of change

7/18/2024 Jersey City, NJ, USA

David A. Folds

Soft Sleep

my lady still asleep

eyes closed

mouth partly opened

peace of the moment

life's pitfalls away

somewhere else

innocence floating

in a river of dreams

I would not wake her

I would not disturb

the flow

the streams of consciousness

drifting in and out

some to soothe

some to warn

some to reconnect

to past moments

and loved ones gone

when she is awake

quickly

active awareness

will wipe the focus

away from

those dreams

life proceeds inevitably

whether cruel or calm

5/8/2023 Jersey City, NJ, USA

David A. Folds

Gathering

always

      seems a fleeting wish

a concept

      to be desired

but with an unfathomable

      lack of understanding

we connect moments

      for a lifetime

trying to remember

      to reexperience

trying to collate

the past

into a unified

conceptual entity

that contains the tiniest

bit of all time

to label the passage

of our journey

to find peace

within our small

trip to short time

6/24/2023   Jersey City, NJ, USA

David A. Folds

When All Stood Still

sipping coffee

    starting an office day

ensconced in my small piece

    of a large room of desks

all of a sudden

    a banging booming sound

exploded in our space

    the source entirely unknown

then someone announced

    a plane had plunged

        into the Trade Tower

rushing to the windows

    all could see the smoke

        already floating

but nothing to do

    but return to my desk

until again a loud

exploding sound appeared

followed by

word that a second

had hit the other Tower

this time on view

were hundreds of white

paper floating in air

blasted east towards the river

on their way

to Brooklyn

here in Police Headquarters

quickly

speakers

demanded immediate

evacuation

David A. Folds

an act of

      natural caution

who knew what else

      could occur

we all stood outside

      in shock

      in the Plaza

waiting for

      we knew not what

until word passed

      cops to be gathered

      civilians go home

walking northwest

       I just missed seeing

the collapse

       of the West Tower

seeing a mass of mess

       fallen and floating

              above the ground

in a short bit of time

       the East Tower

       followed

while I was getting

       a gourmet sandwich

on Sullivan Street

       at Melampo's

nothing for me to do

       but climb the stairs

       to home

David A. Folds

early next morning

radio and one working

TV station

said those like me should

return to work

from the west edge of Soho

I could walk south

but the smoke flowing

from both wrecks

was in the street

I went East to avoid

the direct pollution

at every corner

every intersection

at least four cops

local or state

or National Guard

or military reserves

checked credentials

to allow to continue

or not

it seemed something like Europe

out of a late 1940s

post war film

I walked from block to block

with ID hanging

clearly displayed

from checkpoint to checkpoint

until reaching the building

communication was minimal

but work resumed

alive but wrapped

into a many shared

shock of sorrow

8/11/2023 Jersey City, NJ, USA

David A. Folds

Intrusion

write the words

     ready or not

the impulse demands

     exposure

a phrase imposing

     importance

like the blare of headlights

     in a dark night space

why does it survive

     unlike other lost

          floating thoughts

I must travel with

and past it

to find what riches

can be uncovered

and displayed

is it a map that leads

to treasures

or to a useless swamp

of drivel in wasted time

9/23/2023   Jersey City, NJ, USA

25   David A. Folds

10th Month

October lacks

    the punch of Spring

the leaves are lost

    or past decline

the branches half

    or totally naked

as breezes spread

    the cooling air

and coats and hats

    have found their time

intense summer heat

    vanished into calm

but winds can start

    to push against us

cold can reach right

       through our clothes

still any and everything

       now is possible

the clock is ticking

       and the Gods look down

to see what may transpire

       what tries to spread your wings

10/23/2023   Jersey City, NJ, USA

David A. Folds

Vickie in Hospital

I can not measure the affect

    of her being

        to my psyche

but I know my being

        is not always receptive

although I think vibrations

        penetrate even then

our communications

        have come in words

in looks in gestures

        in facial expressions

in touches and kisses

        and sometimes further

now

I talk to her

and look with love

her eyes look to mine

to seek a psychic touch

I feel - I hope - she absorbs

all the love

I can send her

her sweetness always

touches me

deep within

11/10/2023 Jersey City, NJ, USA

David A. Folds

Reflections

when looking back

in time

it all seems a mystery

flowing out of

a white cloud

of smoke

but then still

I can almost

reach out a hand

and touch the past

echoes in

a curtain of mist

faintly heard

wiped away

when the moment

claims attention

and each second

demands it's due

am I not the one

    who laughed as a child

who cried as a baby

    and puzzled at the advent

        of sexual awakening

eventually discovering

    a lifetime mate

a quiet soul

    a special sweetness

I am not the only one

    appreciating this

but am the most receiving

    the most lucky

    of all her friends

we both chose

    to choose

    to bond together

selection for a lifetime

    whatever comes our way

12/28/2023 Jersey City, NJ, USA

David A. Folds

Sand

I only know the sand

    from the shore

        and that in an hourglass

the harshness of the desert

    is only an image

        or an idea for me

a child's sandbox

    substitute for a beach

        was a youngsters' playground

I'm told the origins

    of circumcision

was to avoid sand

    in the foreskin

we hear of danger

    of dreaded quicksand

life lost as sand slips away

    like a gaping mouth

sandpaper scrapes away

    the roughness of wood

to smooth the irregularities

    in the adventure of living

while we wander the flow

    of sand dunes

      close to the shore

to lose the love

    of sorrow

2/9/2024 Jersey City, NJ, USA

David A. Folds

Flowing Forward

when the wind

    was young

and the mountains

    were tolerant

the oceans frolicked

    and laughed

birds and insects

    flew as pollinators

while streams drifted

    on to nowhere

and lakes and ponds

    sat almost in silence

we were innocent

    and full of questions

waiting to see

    we knew not what

wishing to find

    tomorrow today

the days progressed

    and regressed

faults forgiven

    foolishness too frequent

David A. Folds

the flowers ebbed

and flowed

the trees lived

on for ever

and we grew and

flourished boldly

without a grip

on larger spirit

with moments lost

among moments

and trivia mixed

within essentials

until a quietness

was found

and peace was in

the breeze of Spring

2/15/2024   Jersey City, NJ, USA

Inquiry

when the light refuses to dim

the quiet in the shadows

    looks for some resurgent energy

nowhere to be found

    and calm passes through

to answers never given

    questions never asked

static being

    lost in retrogression

time passes forward

    it's all it can do

how to dance

    to the song of the light

how to swim

    in the energy of its heat

how to find a pathway

    to its brightness

6/13/2024 Jersey City, NJ, USA

David A. Folds

Regression

sunshine lost

    in the ripples of the river

the day creeps forward

    reluctantly

moments forgotten

    before they start

how have we

    come to this

the sky floats dripping

    cloud formations

the mist hovers

    in a last hurrah

your existence has

     reached an impasse

I feel the confusion

     all the frustration

your body deep in a

     halting quagmire

progressive not a

     positive this time

moments passing

     wishes gone with them

but the rays of early sunlight

     flex their muscles

continuing to warm the energy

     into the breath of life

2/15/2024 Jersey City, NJ, USA

David A. Folds

Easter Sadness

drink no more from this cup

my darling

bitter taste flows through every

ounce inside

now no more sweet manna

pleasing taste

refuse all the needed

nourishment

Parkinson's pushes back

needs and wants

perspectives ignoring

healing growth

lost in retrogression

losing weight

a spoon fed offering

    all refused

nurses patience strained

    try again

locked teeth you don't want it

    please my dear

accept some energy

    tasteless food

fading hope for regrowth

    can it be

David A. Folds

look for life continued

but less able

to do those basic things

you assumed

were easy every day

now are lost

into prone inertia

frustration

boundless every second

how can you

feel moment to moment

how can you

love the gift of living

living less

now God's blessing testing

you and me

3/31/2024   Jersey City, NJ, USA

Lost

when my mother died

      I didn't cry

she was ninety-seven

      with late Alzheimer's

a shadow of her

      younger being

I didn't cry

      for my father

who passed from a blessed

      creative life

he too was ninety-seven

      assisted living toward

            the end of his time

David A. Folds

I saw more of my brother's

    deep decline

never fat he had become

    frightenly skinny

        during Covid's curse

lungs damaged

    hard to breath

impossible to play his

    inspiring jazz piano

for more than a year's span

    he suffered more

        in mind than body

I listen to his records

    missing him

unable to have done something

to give him recovery

and any hope

reading a poem

about his loss

could not stop

dropped tears

down my face

but my own darling

began her decline

of over four years

and we didn't know

what was happening

when we did

she was very restricted

David A. Folds

finally diagnosed

    as Parkinson's

fully dependent

    I tried to assist

but a long journey in

    and out of hospitals

dominated my time and

    became her existence

over her last year

    unable to speak

      barely to move

consciousness

    wrapped inside

attended, needled,

    fed and washed

she could look and listen

    but communication

      was gone

the fifteen to twenty years

    we expected to share

flown away

    without a word

moments of grief

    will come and go

but a partner of life

    had to pass on

and leave her widower

    at a loss to recover

half of his existence

    gone and buried

    in a grave

8/17/2024 Jersey City, NJ, USA

David A. Folds

Found in Two Lost Years

it seemed to be a different version

of the same day throughout

most of two years

do all the morning

preparations

before breakfast

have the same food with

my home-made coffee

most of two years

finish everything else

to be ready to leave

down to the building's lobby

to raise the Uber app

directed to her hospital

watching variations of routes

seeing one slightly faster

this day perhaps

sign in at reception

        which reads my temperature

           from my wrist

elevator up to her floor

        her ward

           to her room
place my coat and bag

        on one chair to be free

           to come to her bedside

a smile

        a good morning

           my love

a kiss

        with a slight response

           from her lips

an orienting

        informing list

           of today's now

David A. Folds

what day is it

      what is happening later

or tomorrow

      that is particular

how is the weather outside

      from her closed window

            which she can barely see

check that the machines

      are not beeping

that she seems

      as comfortable as can be

talk with the nurse

      has she been stable

sit with her

      talk to her

            sometimes read to her

in the afternoon

      have my same sandwich

accompanied

      by water also from home

decide what time to leave

and talk about that

giving a heartfelt kiss

goodnight

always telling her

I love her now

and for all eternity

leaving with a bottled up

sadness

needing my time

to rest

and rejuvenate

to be her lifeline of love

and perhaps some hope

improbable as it may be

5/31/2024   Jersey City, NJ, USA

David A. Folds

Love and Time

only time can move

      the mighty mountains

but quickly swallows

      our wisp of life

within a grain of

      celestial existence

we radiate internal

      energy quietly

connecting with other

      humans sometimes

love becomes the

      highest communication

impossible to measure

      amazing to acquire

value not always

      fully understood

I have learned that

    its lasting power

transcends the loss

    of earthly breath

love that we cannot

    touch or measure

existing somewhere

    wrapped in quiet

radiating

    inside always

like the unseen

    explosion of an atom

4/30/2024 Jersey City, NJ, USA

David A. Folds

Retreat Center

a small clearing between

the cluster of trees

allows the sun to declare

its interrupted intentions

while leaves fidget and sway

to the dance of the moving air

a few trees partially bare

display the chaos

of empty branches

their growth seemed to have

no sense of direction

an abstract intrusion

into reality

down the hills different paths

    give choices to be made

back to the Chapel

    down to a designed maze

off to the animals

    visit an active vegetable garden

or return to the main building

    to rest and ruminate

the blessings stack on top of

    blessings for now

7/13/2024 West Cornwall, CT, USA

David A. Folds

Art

the moon half swallowed

     by uncaring floating clouds

presents a Van Gogh

     evolving cluster like paint

in and out

     of a starless night

wrapped in quiet peace

     that breathes to slow the pulse

no camera steals each moment

     paintings moving before my eyes

captured not on canvas

     but echoed in my breath

oxygen spreading

     throughout my veins

slowly quiet moments

     become the future

without any help of mine

7/13/2024 West Cornwall, CT, USA

Guernica

in the sixties

     in the chaos of the times

a visit to MOMA

     transformed space and balance

then Picasso's Guernica

     owned a dynamic wall

chaos contained

     in a glorious rectangle

all the variations

     of confusion and terror

captured in blacks

     and whites and greys

we read from the left

     crossing towards a margin

David A. Folds

but this piece flows

     forcefully from the right

towards a mother

     cradling her dead child

crying in hysteria

     up to the impersonal sky

while a dying victim

     lies stretched out below

and a bull's bust looks on

     in stoic lack of concern

the power of the painting

     contained within its boundaries

declares the painter's protest

    and sits within our mind

glory of a creation

    echoing still inside us

and September 10, 1981

    loomed for me and others

as the painting on loan

    had to be returned to Spain

11/16/2024 Jersey City, NJ, USA

David A. Folds

Playing

out the north facing

    living room window

directly across

    balconies with lounge chairs

        sitting alone unoccupied

below to the right

    the park-like tiled space

where three pickleball courts

    live in a line filled ellipse

in the winter season

    it will be transformed

      into a skating rink

      not for free

but now

    with absence of rain

        courts fully occupied

more enthusiasts

    wait their time

        to show their mediocrity

8/92024 Jersey City, NJ, USA

David A. Folds

Brightness

smiling eyes

    that laughed within

        the moment's pleasure

captivating anyone

    luckily observing

her serious or troubled lips

    forgotten with upturned

        blissful cheeks

all she wanted was peaceful

    group inclusion

to interact with

    social bonding

except to me where

    bonding was unending

        with ebbs and flows

        inevitable

but those moments

when eyes and cheeks

showed full energy of loving

reverberate

within me

still today

8/142024   Jersey City, NJ, USA

David A. Folds

Transient

I was a child

    of the true December

grown old in winds

    that don't forgive

cold greeting the first

    necessary doctor's slap

more snow before

    our current warming

New England piled it

    higher than a small child

who was protected

    from the weather of life

seasons declared

    their demanding character

four periods

    defining which clothes

which sports

    required attention

summer sun bleached

    our skin 'til red

piles of degrading leaves announced

    the advent of autumn

wind-blown snow sparkled

    in the winter sun

then the softened earth opened

    to embrace the showers of spring

and the young blossomed

    in tune with awakening nature

while I watched generations

    climb and stumble

rapt in the continuum of challenges

    outside of my cocoon

8/16/2024   Jersey City, NJ, USA

David A. Folds

The Flow of Time

when I look back

    to lost moments in time

small cinema like images

    peek through a diaphanous curtain

        too briefly flirtatious

and then gone pushed aside

    by rude reality

all the hours and years

    hinted at this

        demanded at that

and their times were

    only stepping stones

above a river

    requiring recognition

flowing every which way

faster than we could react

sometimes we slipped

off those stones

caught in a powerful rush

helplessly confused

hopelessly drowning

until regaining solid surface

to continue in our

myopic life style

while the vast ocean of life

brought wave upon wave

flowing --- ignorant

of our existence

8/24/2024 Jersey City, NJ, USA

David A. Folds

Rising

dawn bring me more

than light

bright red to orange

onto yellow

floats across

the eastern horizon

demanding attention

to all not shuttered down

when I still was working

I would peep

through the slats

experiencing morning's

declarations

before attending

to today's demands

seeing if this rise

deserved some photos

Nature original artist

for us all

river flowing south

early sailboat

decorating accent

to the wide Hudson

moments to gather camera

capturing the slightest

bit of time

what is next

what will serve

to match the beauty

of this dawn

9/13/2024 Jersey City, NJ, USA

David A. Folds

Time and Space

my place has not

    expanded

but the sense of space

    certainly has

it was an overflow of

    accumulation before

some mine

    some hers

had almost reached

    a choking point

and with her gone now

    also would be her stuff

opening walking

    even exercising space

but after over

    forty years

with a small one

    with such big love

filling the void

    of uncertain self

the emptiness speaks

    without a word

and the time

    cries out to flow

inside a single life

    unused to this

    newest loneliness

9/19/2024 Jersey City, NJ, USA

David A. Folds

Lonely Night

all is quiet

      except the TV

outside barely

      a sound to hear

no blaring car stereo

      passing by

the space inside

      contains me like

            a floating cocoon

I sit to see,

      to eat, to read

but I say nothing

      and no one's there

      to reply

how to fill the energy

    implied by

        a missing mate

the longer I remain awake

    the emptiness

        echoes silently

until I finally force

    myself to sleep

9/29/2024 Jersey City, NJ, USA

David A. Folds

Smoke

the wind rushes

    to judge the moment

gone before the rush

    can manage to escape

as time floats

    in confusion

looking back at what

    has fled beyond

that flits away

    into foggy mist

we are mere microbes

in the morning

a microsecond's

dance in space

forgotten and forgiven

forever

where the wind fades off

into the night

10/2/2024 Jersey City, NJ, USA

David A. Folds

Half

living in the

    tyranny of time

moments fly away

    in receding echoes

past connections haunt

    an unforgiving evening

the quiet insists that nothing

    else is happening

as you are a prisoner

    wrapped in nowhere

what more can you do

    to find a rhythm of balance

now half of you is gone

      lost in her buried ashes

your total identity so married

      to a shared duality

but you remain alone

      still retaining cosmic breath

is it time to reinvent

      a better half

can you rediscover

      your fully vibrant being

lost moments forever gone

      as now demands its due

10/24/2024 Jersey City, NJ, USA

David A. Folds

Memorial

the picture speaks to me

    each time I pass by

an enlargement

    from thirty years ago

mounted on a cardboard base

    sitting upright quietly

we were dining at our

    favorite SoHo hangout

Italian pasta and pizza

    in a small space on Spring Street

as luck would have it

    I had my camera

and luck said she would

    give a beautiful smile

but it was reserved and peaceful

    trusting my photographic skill

the enlargement was ordered

    for her memorial

it did its duty

    now the memory is tweaked

each time I pass it

    blowing forth a kiss

11/21/2024 Jersey City, NJ, USA

David A. Folds

Before the Fullness of Time

the river remembers

always

to forget faithfully

in the calm

of a windless morning

or in the turmoil of white tips

moments come and gone

the flow presents saltwater

back towards mother ocean

a rolling ebbtide

pushing outward slowly

cleaned of past pollution

again alive with fish to eat

Henry Hudson could not imagine

the future shoreline buildings

once it was nature's untouched

       pristine purity

then

       Manhattan's water's edge

             was much further inward

now the land has expanded

       with constructed projections

while a barge is guided and urged

       by its small power boat

a pleasure liner lit with energy

       sounds its warning

peace implied

       upon the shore

calm supposed

       cold culture from the shoreline

David A. Folds

in a late November

    metamorphosis

naked trees in stark

    embarrassment

helplessly dance

    in the cold cruel wind

no leaves for growth now

    no photosynthesis

only the gift of precipitation

    feeds the needs of roots

until winter frozen earth

    blocks subterranean access

these lofty beings

    hibernate outside

surviving as usual

    stoic beyond humanity

taken for granted

    by busy passing persons

past early dawn

    the sky blossomed

into a cushion

    of pastel blue

a painter's brush flowing forth

    accents of cirrus clouds

delicate amorphous

    floating streaks

dancing through the solar

    penetrating rays

David A. Folds

our drama plays the game

of moments

pretending all the trivia

is truly important

watching lower cumulus

slowly claim the sky

until evolving into aggressive

cumulonimbus

clouds with a purpose

to wash and cleanse us

a new dense darkness

releasing a downpour

we run for cover

    chased by fury

awaiting a change

    a release from dominance

a dark deluge shifts

    slanting wind gusts

we back in further

    into the overhang

soaked in coldness

    below the knees

waiting for time

    to free us

      from the storm

David A. Folds

we watch the moments

    lost and interrupted

forgetting how this wash

    bestows its love

so fully baptizing

    with its brush

after the deluge

    out from shelter

stepping away from

    the deeper puddles

rivulets of rainwater

    stream down

        every decline

Lost - Trying to Find Anew

wet as may be

relieved but unhappy

we forget to recognize

the moment's magic

the quiet truth

even among the smallness

the minus and the plus

we're still standing on

sacred ground

12/1/2024 Jersey City, NJ, USA

David A. Folds

Playing the Role

dawn is not the beginning

    daylight opens the second act

and we slept peacefully

    on through the entire first

more truant than vagrant

    nothing supersedes our slumber

the stage has rotated overnight

    spotlights were reset

we rise without a stage applause

    rapt in we know not what

slowly ruminating

    towards the bathroom

looking for some relief

    no chance to earn a Tony

12/19/2024 Jersey City, NJ, USA

Holiday Growing Up

family gathering Christmas Day

growing up in Evanston

always special with the spread

much the same

the entire meal better

than any dining out

four families of one generation

each with at least one junior

hosted by grandparents

seated at either end

of the large

dining room table

David A. Folds

fattened roasted turkey stuffed

    with a usual family recipe

gravy just right

    cranberry to add an accent

mashed potatoes

    topped with that gravy

vegetables there

    but not the focus

a good wine for those

    already past puberty

conversation about whatever

    only politics proved sticky

always two baked pies

    one of them mince

then a digestive and

    a variety of raw nuts

almost enough nutcrackers

    to go around

most challenging were always

    the large Brazil nuts

scattered bits of shells

    spread for later clean up

first a turkey was stuffed

    now it became our turn

12/21/2024 Jersey City, NJ, USA

David A. Folds

Wind

the wind is the story

>but the plot is a mystery

a diaphanous dance

>with no solid substance

partner to the swaying

>leaves and branches

a flirting brush

>across our faces

a touch one moment

>and gone the next

too fast to be a partner

>away before a kiss

bringing the growing cold

>drawing humidity and heat

when the force surges

    is it declaring its rage

in the calm of stillness

    is it seeking some peace

we really only know that

    we step into its world

12/27/2024 Jersey City, NJ, USA

David A. Folds

"New Openings" on page 1 was intended to be included in my first book of poetry, "Sights, Sounds, and Spirit", but somehow it was omitted. It has been read in open mic readings, but this is its first printing.

David A. Folds

Index of Poems by Titles

David A. Folds